THiS bOOK iS d
SUSie, Laura, EMbeY & L…n

FUN-SCHOOLING WITH
IMAGINATION
The Storytelling Book

HOW TO USE THIS BOOK:
Look at the beautiful pictures
and make up your own stories.
Choose one picture each day.
Record your story.

Kaltes Roastbeef

- rosa gebraten -
mit
Bratkartoffeln
und sauce
Remoulade
15,80

Photography by Joshua Brown
& Sarah Janisse Brown
Animal Adventures
In Switzerland, Italy & Germany

Made in United States
Orlando, FL
08 December 2024

54821274R00077